Latimer Briefing 18

Commemorating War and Praying for Peace

A Christian Reflection on the Armed Forces

by John Neal

The Latimer Trust

CONTENTS

1. Foreword

The chronic inability of humans to get along with one another has ensured that history is dominated by a diary of nearly constant armed conflict. Despite the march of so-called civilization, the increasing destructiveness of modern weaponry, to say nothing of weapons of mass destruction (WMD), meaning nuclear, chemical and bacteriological weapons, means that the potential for casualties and the wastage of modern war are vastly greater than those of centuries ago, while the recently ended 20th century must be on record as among the bloodiest of them all.

While the threat of the Cold War, with its so-called nuclear 'peace' reinforced by 'mutually assured destruction' (appropriately enough labelled "MAD") has receded, at least the protagonists of that phase of international relations could be relied upon to be more or less rational and able to understand one another's thought processes. However, though the Cold War has now receded into history, the 21st century still contains WMD (for, much and all as we'd like to, they cannot be 'un-invented'), and the possibility that they may one day arm fundamentalist religious or other extremist groups with very narrow political viewpoints, and which excuse 'terror' operations under the pretext that it is God's will (if not God's direct command), means that our modern world remains just as dangerous if not more so thanks to the added factors of political and religious extremism and volatility.

So, as we commemorate the centenary of World War One, optimistically but naively labelled at the time as 'the war to end all wars', well might we pray that indeed, it might have so been!

This booklet sets out first to describe the place and role of armed forces and the 'Just War' theory, some of the pressures under which personnel of the modern Western world's militaries serve as well as some of the moral issues surrounding the existence and the use of these same forces. It spends some time discussing the place of Christians in the military and the role of chaplains as God's servants and witnesses within it. Finally it makes some observations and suggestions about commemoration ceremonies, both of wars in general and individual battles in particular, all especially pertinent as we live through the centenary of World War 1. However, rather than a deep theological work, this booklet contains more the personal reflections of one who spent 23 years as a chaplain of the Royal New Zealand Air Force

(RNZAF), latterly as the Principal Chaplain of the New Zealand Defence Force, and thus the perspective is that gained during those years. This should always be borne in mind, for the practices and cultures of other countries' military forces are not necessarily those of this small Pacific nation but, where differences are known, they are mentioned.

Beyond observing that armed conflict is a product of the weaknesses of sinful human beings, especially those of fear, ambition, expediency or a lust for power, this booklet does not touch upon the causes of war. The author is more than content to leave that to the historians, theologians and philosophers. Nor does it delve very deeply into efforts made to understand war, how it might be prevented or how "Just War Theory" provides a degree of Christian justification of armed conflict, or how the Geneva Conventions seek to ameliorate its worst aspects. These are all large topics in themselves to say nothing of being well beyond the author's competence to discuss in any depth.

Blenheim

New Zealand

February 2015

2. War and Peace

How should Christians deal with military service?

There has always been debate both for and against the place of military forces and, even if they should be determined to be necessary, whether or not Christians should serve within their ranks. Of course these are important issues for all thoughtful people, but it is often very hard to discuss them in any dispassionate manner in which light does not eventually give way to heat. Feelings can run very high, and in my mind are well remembered scenes from the huge demonstrations that took place protesting against the Viet Nam war, to say nothing of the irony of much violence at that time being perpetrated in the name of peace.

2.1. *Security and safety of citizens*

That said, it is generally accepted that one of the first duties of any state is to take all reasonable steps to ensure the security and safety of its citizens. Thus to that end they have Police Forces which are charged with maintaining internal security against crime and unrest. In the same manner, almost every sovereign state also has its armed defence forces to provide for external security. These comprise highly disciplined personnel trained to wage armed conflict should that ever be deemed necessary or, just as importantly, are seen to be equipped and ready to do so. Some states are too tiny and too poor to provide for their own defence but do so in alliance with neighbouring states, an example of this being the Cook Islands, Niue and the Tokelau Islands of the south-west Pacific Ocean, all looking to New Zealand for their physical security. In the same way, nations large and small frequently ally their forces with those of other nations to provide a greater collective strength, examples being the North Atlantic Treaty Organisation (NATO), the Five Power Defence Arrangement (FPDA) and the now defunct Warsaw Pact to name but a few. Political expediency can also encourage nations to form shorter-term alliances during major conflicts, subsequently to leave them or even to switch sides. A typical and relatively recent example is Japan, allied to Great Britain and other allies during World War I but their formidable adversary during World War II.

While most nations seek to resolve their differences with others by peaceable means through diplomacy, there can come times when this fails and so, to quote Carl von Clausewitz's writing in the early 19th century, "War is the continuation of politics by other means."[1]

Thus most nations view the need to raise and maintain armed forces as a sad necessity of life, given that we live in a fallen world in which, as St Paul pointed out,

> .....the whole Creation has been groaning as in the pains of childbirth right up to the present time. (Romans 8:22).

They would love to devote the money spent on recruiting, training and equipping their armed forces to more positive sectors of modern life, but the day in which they feel they can do that has yet to dawn. Even if a nation might feel physically secure against direct invasion, the maintenance of forces to provide for a wider regional security are usually thought necessary. As an example, New Zealand has little realistic fear of direct invasion of her shores for, by virtue of its location in the south-west Pacific Ocean, it is protected by the largest moat in the world. However, the south-west Pacific region is far from secure, and as large nations jostle for influence in the area, as tensions over such places as the Spratley Islands (claimed by some five nations at last count) simmer just below the surface and even as fishing resources face threats, neither Australia nor New Zealand can snooze contentedly in their small corner of the world as if they are immune from what happens all around them.

2.2. Peacekeeping forces

While most defence forces are so named because they are commonly seen to act as barriers to hostile invasion, they can also play a direct role in peace-keeping duties anywhere, making the world generally a safer place for everyone, while at the other end of the continuum, armed forces personnel, given their training and discipline, are invaluable for giving aid to their governments in times of national emergencies such as floods, earthquakes, internal security and the containment of disease outbreaks.

---

[1]   Carl Von Clausewitz, *On War* (Princeton: Princeton University Press Translation, 1976), Chapter 1, Section 24.

Consequently, many armed forces personnel are engaged upon what is loosely called 'peacekeeping', a term which covers a whole range of military activities. At one extreme is 'peace making', in which they may actively intervene between two warring antagonists by force of arms or else drive out an invader, while at the other they provide a social stability and security in the form of an 'iron fist in a velvet glove', that is, armed troops whose stance is neutral and whose loyalty cannot be bought, keeping factions apart to allow rank and file citizens to get on with their lives until the civil mood removes the causes or the climate in which violent differences can take place.

A recent example of the former would be the role of the Coalition Forces in chasing Iraq's Saddam Hussein out of Kuwait, while a positive example of the latter would be the combined Australian and New Zealand operation in the Solomon Islands. This was essentially a police operation, but military forces of both (and other Pacific) countries provided an armed back-up against situations which escalated beyond police resources. The military also carried out highly visible patrols, moving through villages and among the general population, getting to know them and making friends with them, a process known as 'hearts and minds'. Often, this kind of presence is all that is required to ensure general peace and stability, for people are reassured that the soldiers are only on the side of law and order and are there to provide a defence against thuggery and crime.

While all troops thus engaged carry weapons and the magazines of those weapons will contain their quota of live ammunition, maybe it is not generally known that the soldier is taught five stages of operational readiness for them, to suit the many situations they can face. The first state is the very non-threatening slinging of the rifle over the soldier's back with the muzzle pointing down. The second state of readiness is to have the rifle still slung over the shoulder but in front of the soldier, again with the muzzle pointing to the ground. Next comes the carrying of the rifle in both hands across the chest, a much more alert state, followed by the cocking of the weapon but keeping the muzzle in the air and then, at the final and most belligerent stage, the aiming of a cocked weapon ready for immediate fire.

Peacemakers may well feel they have to maintain at least the third state of readiness, while peacekeepers would use the first state as much as possible, that is if they are armed in the first place. For example, during the tensions and riots in the Papua New Guinea island of Bougainville during the early 1990s, troops deployed there were unarmed, their moral strength being thought (thankfully accurately) to be sufficient to start bringing peace to that region.

2.3. Christians and the Forces

Of course, the place of Christians within such forces remains a moot point. One school of thought maintains that, as the Armed Forces are 'killing machines', Christians should have no part in them, for their profession is to follow Jesus Christ, the 'Prince of Peace'. Some would cite the examples of the first century Christians in the Roman Legions who often had a very hard time at the hands of their comrades in arms. However, closer study reveals their difficulties were not caused by their profession of arms but by the requirement of Roman soldiers to worship the Emperor as part of their military duties, an idolatrous act they, as Christians, could not do. John the Baptist advised soldiers inquiring how they should respond to his warnings to repent simply to cease from extortion and to be content with their wages (Luke 3:14). It is also pointed out that not even the 'Prince of Peace' Himself counselled the Roman soldiers he met to leave the Army, but more about that later.

St Augustine (354 – 480), Theologian, Philosopher and Bishop of Hippo (in modern day Algeria) was an influential early Christian writer who gave the world some early inklings of what is known as 'The Just War Theory' in an effort to guide military ethics. He was one of the first to assert that a Christian could be a soldier and serve God and country honorably. He claimed that, while individuals should not resort immediately to violence, God has given the sword to governments for good reason (see Romans 13). The purpose of the doctrine is to ensure war is morally justifiable through a series of criteria, all of which must be met for a war to be considered just. The criteria are split into two groups: "the right to go to war" (*jus ad bellum*) and "right conduct in war" (*jus in bello*). The first concerns the morality of going to war and the second with moral conduct within war. Subsequent to Augustine there have been calls for the inclusion of a third category – (*jus post bellum*) – dealing with the morality of post-war settlement and reconstruction, in other words, having won a war, how may a victor then win the peace?

In his turn, Thomas Aquinas (1225 – 1274) used the authority of Augustine's arguments to suggest the conditions under which a war could be considered just:

- ❖ First, just war must be waged by a properly instituted authority such as the state. (Proper Authority is first for it represents the common good which is peace for the sake of man's true end – God.)
- ❖ Second, war must occur for a good and just purpose rather than for self-gain.
- ❖ Third, peace must be a central motive even in the midst of violence. (Right Intention: an authority must fight for the just reasons it has expressly claimed for declaring war in the first place. Soldiers must also fight for this intention.)

Consequently, in going to war justly (*Jus ad Bellum*) a nation needs to consider

- ❖ Just Cause (ie: the reason for going to war must be just),
- ❖ Comparative Justice (ie: the injustice suffered by one party must greatly outweigh that of the other)
- ❖ Competent Authority (ie: it must be declared by a lawful Government),
- ❖ Right Intention (only to right a wrong),
- ❖ Probability of Success (disproportionate means are not permitted),
- ❖ Last Resort (all peaceful means have been exhausted), and
- ❖ Proportionality (anticipated benefits must outweigh anticipated harms).

Then, in conducting a war justly, (*Jus in Bello*) political and military authorities need to consider:

- ❖ Distinction (distinguish between combatants and non-combatants),
- ❖ Proportionality (ie: the harm caused to non-military targets and people must not outweigh military benefits),
- ❖ Military Necessity (again, this refers to confining combat to military targets as much as possible),
- ❖ Prisoners of War (must be regarded as non-combatants and treated humanely), and
- ❖ No Means (no use to be made of inhumane weapons such as rape, torture or weapons of mass destruction).

Further discussion of this matter is beyond the scope of this booklet and the reader is referred to many excellent, detailed and thoughtful books which examine the matter thoroughly, particularly Bishop Tom Frame's *Living by the Sword – The Ethics of Armed Intervention* (UNSW Press, 2004).

3. The Roles of Military Chaplains

From the Christian perspective, military chaplains are priests, clergy, pastors in uniform. They are properly ordained ministers of their respective denominations, they remain in good standing within those denominations and, in uniform, they perform all the duties that would be expected of them by their parent churches plus all the extra ones they inherit from the military.

3.1. Missionaries in uniform

But before we get into the minutiae of just what that means, military chaplains are, primarily, *missionaries of Jesus Christ in uniform*. Not only have they felt called by God the Holy Spirit into the ordained ministry, but they also have received a further call into the armed services to serve Jesus Christ within their ranks. Of course, their primary motive should, as with all of Christ's followers, lie with His Great Commission as recorded in Matthew 28:18-20 and Mark 16:15. Jesus told them to '...go into all the world...to make disciples...', a world which must include that of the military. While this inclusion is somewhat conjectural in the minds of some Christians (though not so for one person who, in writing to a Church newspaper, hotly declared, "I definitely know it is <u>not</u> God's will that chaplains should be in the military!") the fact remains that the military contains men and women for whom Christ died on the cross and that His Great Commission's aims are directed as much to them as it is to civilians. This Commission to Jesus' original disciples were His final words to them during His time on earth and their echo continues through all subsequent history to the present day and continues to motivate the members of His church in all that they do, including those whose ministries are in the military.

On a somewhat more prosaic note, the British Army's *Kings Regulations* put it this way, (but notice that even these dry words include the duties of '... religious instruction and welfare of the officers and soldiers and of the families.'):

> The duties to be performed by a chaplain include the Sunday services, baptisms, churchings, funerals, attending the sick in hospital and reading prayers with the convalescents, visiting soldiers under sentence in military prisons or detention barracks at least once a week.....besides attending generally to the religious

instruction and welfare of the officers and soldiers and of the families.

Chaplains will be treated with the respect due to their rank and profession, and COs will render them every assistance in carrying out their duties.[1]

My reading tells me that the earliest military chaplains not only led the prayers, they also led the charge. Their role was to carry their side's 'totem' or standard onto the battlefield to act as the rallying point and to be the inspiration to their troops. If, in the scheme of things, the appearance of the totem also discouraged the enemy's troops, so much the better. However, it didn't take long for any opponent to work out that the sooner they flattened or otherwise levelled the totem the sooner their opponents would lose all heart, so it didn't take them long to focus their attention upon the chaplain carrying it.

3.2. Incarnational ministry

This leaves one wondering just what chaplain morale was like back in those days, but nowadays they have a more pacific part to play and in today's armed forces they are there primarily in the evangelistic and pastoral roles. They wear the uniform of their parent service (be it Army, Navy or Air Force) and are fully answerable to military law just like any soldier. They receive training in the ethos and culture of their respective Services and are, in every respect, fully commissioned members of them. This is seen to be an important part of 'incarnational ministry' for, while chaplains operate under special military and international rules and are given a degree of independence from their Service's way of operating, they display through their training and their wearing of the uniform, that they are a proper part of the organisation, that they understand what it is like and, to put it prosaically, "...the rain that falls on the head of the common soldier also falls on the head of the chaplain!"

This is an important factor. The chaplain's uniform proclaims full membership of the parent Service and reassures its personnel that he or she understands the way in which it works, the protocols and procedures that must be adopted, as well as the values and culture that are part of each country's military in general, and its individual Services

---

[1] *King's Regulations* for the Army as at the end of World War II.

in particular. In other words, chaplains are, and are seen to be 'One of us' even though they normally do not carry weapons, a matter covered more fully anon.

3.3. *Chaplain's status within the force*

That said and as mentioned above, chaplains operate under special rules. While they hold the Queen's Commission and wear officers' rank insignia (in the Army and the Air Force), their primary badges of 'rank' are the crosses on their shirt collars or shoulders which proclaim their chaplaincy role. That role includes strict neutrality and, to that end, chaplains are stripped of any authority (other than moral authority) implied by the rank insignia they wear. For example, they are not permitted to give orders (only advice), they may not discipline anyone, nor may they sit on Courts Martial. In this way, while they are part and parcel of their parent Service, they are quite deliberately slightly removed from it so as to be seen to have a degree of independence. In return, and to aid the pastoral process, chaplains are relieved from needing to work within the chain of command and are generally free to go where and when they need to in order to perform their duties.

Sometimes this can lead to confusion about whether or not chaplains should, therefore, be saluted. There are two aspects to this question, the first being easily dealt with in that insofar as they have the Queen's Commission, they should be. A salute presented to anyone bearing the Commission does not acknowledge the holder as a person who may be liked or disliked, but the Queen's Commission itself. It might be argued then that this then reinforces a formal barrier to the pastoral relationship but, in the NZDF anyway, most people do not see any requirement to salute as cutting across either the ready access any may have to a chaplain or the informality of private talks with him or her. As a wise colleague once told a class of trainees,

> When we are alone together, either as a class or individually, informality and being able to relax is important. But when we are outside, military protocol demands that we wave to one another in the approved fashion.

The other aspect is what a chaplain should do if, for any reason, a junior officer or a non-commissioned person should go by without proffering a salute. Should this happen to any other class of commissioned officer the result would be at least a verbal reprimand if not a formal charge, but if it involves a chaplain, the wise ones will do and say nothing whatever for, as mentioned two paragraphs ago, they do not have disciplinary powers nor may they issue reprimands. Unwise chaplains have been known to 'chew out' offenders but at the expense of their reputations and they will be – usually correctly – judged either as clots or as *prima donnas* who are of little use unless absolutely necessary. However, it goes without saying that chaplains will always salute a superior officer and must always acknowledge salutes offered to them with a return salute. In the Royal New Zealand Navy, as with its Royal Navy 'Parent Service' where the chaplains do not wear rank insignia, then salutes are neither expected or received.

A further question concerns whether junior chaplains should salute more senior colleagues. My understanding of the British practice is that they do and this usually also applies within the Australian Defence Force, but perhaps because New Zealand is as far away from its "Mother Country" as it is possible to get on this globe, the culture has grown and been accepted that chaplains do not salute one another or use honorifics when talking amongst themselves.

My understanding is that the chaplains of the United States armed forces, (Army, Navy, Air Force and Marines) are given powers of discipline and are thus entitled to give orders. How this works in practice, and what effect it has upon relationships between personnel and their chaplains is not known to me, but suffice to say it appears to work for them and that is the main thing.

A variation of this theme is found in the Royal New Zealand Navy which, like the Royal Navy after which it is patterned, does not give its chaplains any rank insignia, instead giving them the equivalent rank of whomever they happen to be with or talking to. This is illustrated by a well known story in which a new naval chaplain was being interviewed by the Captain of a ship to which he had been appointed. As he turned to leave, the Captain said, "Remember, while you are speaking to me, you are a Captain. When you visit the boiler room and are talking to a stoker, you are a stoker!"

This works within the naval context, given its long tradition of chaplaincy service and the close confines of a ship's company in which the place and the role of the chaplain are clearly understood and, while it has superficial attractions to those in the other two services, there are fishhooks which are not immediately apparent and which properly keep NZ Army and RNZAF chaplains wearing rank insignia.

Whether or not chaplains *should* wear rank insignia is frequently asked, both by (usually) new chaplains as well as by some of their fellow Service men and women. As mentioned, Naval chaplains wear only their chaplain's badges for reasons outlined above, but within the larger Army and Air Force, the issue becomes somewhat more complicated. While some people argue that rank insignia imply privilege (which can be and, sadly, sometimes is abused), they also imply responsibility and duty. A common misconception is that officers simply give orders when, under military law, they are also primarily responsible for the health, the welfare, the competence and the morale of everyone under their command. Just as a captain is held responsible for everything that happens on his or her ship, so every officer is responsible for everything that occurs within his or her Section, Flight, Platoon, Battalion, Squadron etc. Of course, this responsibility also comes with powers of punishment in order to maintain a collective discipline through personal or self-discipline. Of course it is this latter aspect which the general public (to say nothing of the more lowly ranked Service personnel) generally see and think of when confronted with rank, but so important is the former aspect that anyone bearing authority forgets this to the certain detriment of his or her career!

As previously observed, the chaplains of Commonwealth countries receive the Queen's Commission. Upon first enlistment into the New Zealand Defence Force (NZDF) for example, their rank is, officially, Chaplain Class 4 which, in the NZ Army carries the three 'pips' of an Army Captain, its RNZAF equivalent being the two 'medium' bars of a Flight Lieutenant. Usually, once some years of seniority are gained, chaplains are promoted to Chaplain Class Three, thus gaining the Army insignia of the Major's Crown or the 'Scraper Ring' of the Air Force Squadron Leader. The same rank insignia are used in the British Armed Forces and the Australian Defence Force for their 'rank and file' chaplains though their more senior rank levels go much higher in order that they may relate to their proper accountability levels within those much larger forces.

There is good wisdom in giving the majority of chaplains these rank levels. Within each of NZ's three Services the three most junior commissioned ranks (eg: the Air Force's Pilot Officer, Flying Officer and Flight Lieutenant; and the Army's equivalent 2nd Lieutenant, 1st Lieutenant and Captain) are collectively classified as 'Junior Officers' amongst whom is permitted an easy informality. They do not salute one another (except in some ceremonial circumstances) and generally address one another in private by first names. Squadron Leaders (Majors) and above are classed as Senior Officers and the protocols between these rank levels are more rigidly observed. Thus chaplains handily straddle these rank levels, being among either the most senior of the Junior Officers, or a junior Senior Officer, this placing them in the middle order of Commissioned Officers and signifying the relative importance attached to them by their parent services.

In some minds, this rank insignia is a barrier between chaplains and the members of their flock and, indeed, this can happen, especially if the chaplain either takes himself or herself too seriously or else rather likes the look of that insignia in the mirror! On both counts, the careers of such chaplains are usually quite short. On the other side of this coin, some members of the 'flock' have also said it is good to be able to confide in 'someone who has some clout' for it means that a chaplain with much higher rank than they have can speak or act on their behalf! Suffice to say, insofar as chaplains are pastors who are used to working 'with all sorts and conditions of men', his or her approachability and manner soon dismantles any rank barriers.

However, given that military people are also human beings and subject to (sometimes all too) human weaknesses, to say nothing of sinful inclinations, occasionally the status implied by rank insignia can frustrate a chaplain's work. A retired colleague once related how he took a plan of action he felt would assist a pastoral issue within a unit to its Commanding Officer (CO), only to be told, "If you were a Squadron Leader I would listen to your ideas, but since you are a Flight Lieutenant, I will not!" This attitude, fortunately is rare and most chaplains of my experience have had the respect of not just the rank and file but also of their senior officers.

Suffice to say, the Queen's Commission for the chaplains of all three Services, and its attendant rank insignia upon those of the Army and the Air Force simply indicate that chaplains are fully part of the established order and how importantly the parent Service regards their role. For the competent and effective chaplain the rank insignia is unimportant, but for the non-effective chaplain, no amount of rank insignia will help.

As implied by the formal chaplain ranks of the already mentioned Classes Four and Three, there are Chaplains Class Two and Class One. These are simply senior chaplains who have particular leadership roles within chaplaincy itself. Thus a Chaplain Class Two is the Senior Chaplain of his or her parent Service, wears the insignia of the Army's Lieutenant-Colonel or the RNZAF's Wing Commander and is responsible to their respective Service Chiefs for providing the range of chaplaincy services to that Service, while the Principal Defence Chaplain, the one who reports to the Chief of Defence Force, has the lofty title of Chaplain Class One, signalled by their wearing the rank insignia of the Army's Colonel or the Air Force's Group Captain. Of course the Navy's equivalent ranks continue their practice of wearing no insignia at all beyond the common chaplains' badges, no matter what position they hold.

Also, there are equivalent 'rank' structures within all the Commonwealth (and Western Nation) chaplaincies but their differing sizes mean that rank insignia will vary from that of the relatively lowly New Zealand.

3.4. Pastoral role

However, whatever their ranking and position, in the military context, military chaplains are to have time for people, whenever and wherever they are wanted. When people are with a chaplain, whether it is in the chaplain's office, walking together down the road, or sitting around a messdeck table, or quietly talking with one another in the middle of a hangar floor, service people are free to discuss anything under the sun, knowing that they will be listened to, taken seriously, treated respectfully and what they say will be treated in complete confidence. There is no military or civil law which can compel a chaplain to divulge what is said, the sole exception being if the person is contemplating suicide or homicide, for safety of life is paramount. Every Service person has an absolute right to see a chaplain if they feel they wish to, even from within the confines of a cell, but no one can be compelled to see one if they don't. As the saying goes, "All may, none must, but some should!"

This pastoral role takes two general forms. One is generally the more formal presentation of classroom lessons, giving (for example) young trainees skills for living in the Services with their lack of privacy, arduous physical activities and the pressures of discipline; teaching them how to cope with stress; how to resolve differences with other people; how to draw up a personal budget. They also discuss with trainees the problems of negotiating the moral minefields the Services present, such as the bearing of arms, the application of deadly force, the Rules of Armed Conflict and so on. However, even within the formal confines of a military classroom, chaplains will generally be careful to ensure that other unit training (ie. disciplinary) staff are not present so that a less formal atmosphere may prevail and trainees are free to air any collective matters or worries that they feel diffident about broaching through more normal channels. For example, the chaplain could well come from behind the lectern to sit on the corner of a desk and quietly talk to the class just why the drill corporals all seem to act like 'little Hitlers', or why the inspecting officer threw the carefully ironed contents of someone's wardrobe onto the floor, or why the military is much less interested in supporting the bright trainee who coasts through his or her training than in the struggler who, by dint of sheer effort and determination is showing they are really keen to be part of that Service and are putting everything they have into their training.

On a somewhat lighter note, somewhere around week 12 of a 16 week course, a recruit class asked their chaplain when the cold shower regime would cease and the hot water turned on! Given that even a New Zealand winter is cold enough for anybody, the chaplain was quickly able to reassure the class that no such regime existed and the forgotten hot water switch would be promptly turned on. It was. Instant relief!

Informally, the chaplains' roles involve them getting to know, and getting to be known by, the personnel around them. They may meet people out on a hangar floor, in an office, in the Mess, sitting in a ditch on the side of a road during manoeuvres, in their barracks during an evening, or in the unit's hospital, even in the cells!

They are there to be the friend and adviser of everyone, without fear or favour either of rank or position so, consequently, they spend a lot of time counselling, with classroom teaching thrown in on training bases. None of this involves overt religious instruction or Christian witness as such, this being reserved for Chapel Services, out of hours Bible Study groups and such like. Even within counselling situations chaplains have to be sensitive to the needs of the 'client' and not seek to see any session as an evangelistic opportunity. Who the chaplain *is* will commend Christ to secularized people, not what he or she says. To paraphrase St Francis of Assissi, 'Go into all the world and preach the Gospel. Only when absolutely necessary use words!'

3.5. Adviser to command

Which leads to a further role of the chaplain – that of adviser to command. Given the free hand (within reason) chaplains have to roam to and fro around military units, wise commanders rely upon them as their 'eyes and ears' to pass on issues that may arise. This doesn't make the chaplain a breaker of confidences but the adviser of the commander very generally (usually in terms of "No names, no pack-drill") of what is going on. Thus a commander might learn that morale in the unit is very low because all leave has been cancelled and nobody has explained to them why; or that there is a perception in a squad that one of its members is being victimised. Or that sexual harassment is reducing morale and efficiency right through the ship. In the same vein, the chaplain may need to draw upon his or her moral courage to front a commander along the lines of "Sir, what you are saying/doing/contemplating is wrong!"

3.6. Personal qualities

Implicit with their role, the chaplains are so to work as to have the confidence of those below them. This usually isn't very hard, for it simply involves approachability, friendliness, courtesy, a display of respect for all people and a reputation for keeping one's mouth shut. Boiled down, the most basic attribute any chaplain must have is that of Jesus Christ – a genuine love and concern for people. No pastors will be much use if they are indifferent to the human condition for they soon will be seen as cold-hearted and uninterested. If their responses to people's problems and issues appear governed more by form, cliché, text-book quotes or political correctness, then chaplains' insincerity towards people will be all too apparent. Nor will they be good witnesses of Christ if they cannot present the ranks around them with the hope of the gospel, especially in the face of adversity. Academic qualifications and technical competence can never cover over an indifference towards people, for it will readily shine through and make the chaplain remote and unapproachable.

3.7. Confidentiality

Just as important is a reputation for personal discretion. Anything said in confidence to a chaplain has to remain with that chaplain and, as already stated, there is no military or civil law which may compel a chaplain to repeat what has been said to her or him. Of course, a Service person can give the chaplain express permission to take what is said to someone who can effect a change, and often this is the recommended course to take, but even under these circumstances, the chaplain is only free to talk to whomever he or she has been given permission to talk to, and to say only what has been mutually agreed.

Two examples illustrate this. One concerns a newly recruited chaplain who was summoned by a Court Martial to give evidence. The chaplain had expressed reluctance to do so, causing the Court to adjourn for a day and a half while learned counsel debated the issue, but in the end the chaplain was placed in the witness chair. The defendant was eventually found guilty but, upon review by the Court Martial Review Authority (who automatically reviews every case), the conviction was thrown out because, in its opinion, the Court had no right to call upon the chaplain to give evidence.

A second concerns a chaplain of some decades ago who spoke with a Serviceman who was being questioned by the civilian Police about the disappearance of his wife. Her body was not found for many years until the husband eventually led the Police to where he had buried her. Those who knew this chaplain conjectured that he carried the knowledge of this murder for the rest of his life but, because he learned about it only after the event and because of his perception of the circumstances around his reception of any confession, he felt obliged to keep it to himself.

In practical terms, though, many issues related to a military chaplain are easily resolved but only with the involvement of others within that Service. It might be a Private who thinks he may have an STD but is too nervous or shy to take it to the Medical Officer. The chaplain may well offer to accompany the Private to the Medical Section. It might involve an airman in trouble for being late reporting for duty several times in a week. The chaplain might ask for permission to speak to this Airman's CO in very general terms, saying that there are domestic problems at home which means he has to get the children off to school before coming to work, but the problem is being attended to and will soon be fixed. If the airman says that's OK, then the chaplain will have a quiet word with that CO, simply saying there are problems at home he knows about and they'll soon be fixed and that should satisfy the wise CO. An unwise CO will demand to know what the problem actually is but the chaplain, not having the Airman's permission, will tell the CO nothing.

A chaplain's discretion is all important, for without it no-one will come near him or her. Equally important is the confidence of superior officers, for without it, commanders won't listen to or respect their viewpoints. Wise commanders who have confidence in their chaplain(s) will accept what they are advised and not inquire further. As one CO said to the chaplain, "I'd like to know more about this matter but I won't ask, for I know %#@# well you won't tell me!"

A chaplain is effective when troops will readily approach him or her for confidential chats, but is useless if the rank and file keep him or her at a distance. A chaplain is also effective when a CO, hearing he or she is on a case, is relieved and is content to await the outcome. Alternatively, if the CO mutters under his breath and reaches for the worry beads when hearing the same news, then that chaplain is far from effective.

3.8. Faithfulness in the frontline

So far, I have mentioned only human attributes but the chaplain needs much more than just these. If being an ordained minister and a chaplain is just a job, or is 'something nice to do' or is valued for its perceived status, then even if that chaplain has all the above mentioned qualities in spades, they will still lack a fundamental quality – a strong, vibrant and open faith in the Living God. The chaplains' badges symbolise the Cross of Christ and should reflect the personal spiritual qualities and the motivation of each chaplain. For only upon the basis of a close, personal and growing spiritual relationship with God will chaplains remain effective through every situation in which they find themselves for, as with all Christians, it is the Lord God who strengthens and sustains each one in their particular calling and who can, through all circumstances, enable them to remain faithful witnesses to those around them.

While the 'going is good' anyone can do the chaplaincy job to a reasonable degree, but such is military life that the going can easily be anything but good. As well as reminding trainees and troops that their job is essentially unpleasant and dangerous, and they can expect to be placed in situations where every ounce of self-discipline and personal courage will be demanded of them, chaplains need regularly to remind themselves that, insofar as their role is to be with their troops, wherever their troops may be, then precisely the same demands of self-discipline and personal courage will be made of them also. On operations, the chaplain is not called upon to whip up patriotic fervour but is called to be the calm, reassuring presence amongst nervous troops and to help them to stand firm and be strong when faced with every temptation to turn and run.

In the Western Desert during World War II, a unit of the NZ Division was dug in on a low rise and completely surrounded by the Afrika Corps. As troops nervously kept lookout through the night in their foxholes, their chaplain crawled on his stomach, visiting each one through the night to let its occupants know that he was watching and waiting with them.

During World War I, chaplain Geoffrey Studdart-Kennedy was forever to be found in the trenches of the front lines, encouraging and reassuring the soldiers and dispensing from his bulging uniform pockets so many cigarettes that he became forever known as "Woodbine Willie". His conduct was in stark contrast to that of many of his colleagues who contented themselves with remaining largely in the comfort and security of their unit HQs well behind the lines and venturing further forward only when all was quiet. It was such as Woodbine Willy who had the respect and the affection of the soldiers, while many of the latter later reflected bitterly on how they only saw their immaculately uniformed chaplains on rare occasions when all on the front was quiet and safe.

In the military, where everyone is trained to be strong, the chaplain is called to be the strongest of them all. When all else are falling, the chaplain is called to stand, when the noise, the confusion and the danger are all threatening imminent panic, the chaplain is called to be the calming presence which helps those around her or him to be strong and to stand firm. And if wounded troops have to be left behind during a withdrawal, it is the chaplain who stays with them.

In the early hours of February 3, 1943, the US troop transport 'Dorchester' was torpedoed by a U-boat off the coast of Newfoundland. Amongst the 900 or so troops on board were four chaplains. They were Methodist minister the Reverend George L. Fox, Reform-Rabbi Alexander D. Goode (Ph.D.), Roman Catholic priest the Reverend John P. Washington and Reformed Church in America minister the Reverend Clark V. Poling. As the ship drifted without power and began sinking, these four chaplains assisted panicking soldiers and wounded into the lifeboats and, when the life-jackets ran out, surrendered their own to those who did not have them. They then linked arms to sing hymns and to pray as they went down with the ship.

Of all God's servants, chaplains must have the closest relationship with their Lord and their God, for it is He who has called them into the military and it is He whom they serve. They must have the strongest sense of personal call into chaplaincy, and to be ready to make any sacrifice for the sake of those in their care. Theirs is a particularly vulnerable, lonely and demanding calling in which nothing less than the strength God gives will be good enough.

3.9. An armed Chaplain?

A final question for this section is whether or not chaplains should be armed. They serve in armed forces and their personnel are all trained in the effective use of weapons of all kinds. On active operations the personnel of entire units will carry their personal weapons with them all the time, be they rifles or pistols, but what about the chaplain?

The Geneva Conventions state that chaplains must, first and foremost, wear the badge of the non-combatant. In western countries, this is the red cross which is often, but erroneously, thought to be worn only by medical staff. Under the Conventions, this plainly observable badge is meant to denote to both friend and foe that the wearer's role is purely humanitarian and they are not active parts of the fighting arms. These Conventions state that chaplains *may* arm themselves *defensively* to give them some form of self-protection against direct personal threat or to protect sick or wounded under their care. Being armed 'defensively' is generally interpreted as permitting chaplains to carry a pistol, for such weapons are discreet and effective only at very close quarters, the only circumstance in which a chaplain may be permitted to open fire.

That said, many chaplains prefer not to carry weapons at all, for they feel that in being armed they jeopardize their Christian witness, but whenever a military unit 'goes tactical' (ie: with everyone carrying personal weapons on active service), the wise chaplain will discuss with the Commanding Officer whether or not to bear arms. Insofar as the Commanding Officer is responsible for the health, safety and welfare of all under his or her command, he or she needs to feel comfortable with an unarmed chaplain in the unit when considering the nature of the operation, the size and type of the enemy and the tactical situation. Some situations may make the CO quite comfortable with a chaplain exercising a preference to remain unarmed, but others may be deemed so dangerous that an unarmed chaplain would be strictly confined to the defended base camp or headquarters, or else required leave its confines only when accompanied by armed colleagues. This of course can become a burden for the CO and the chaplain but, for the NZDF no chaplain is permitted to carry a rifle. As the rifle is the standard infantry weapon, if it is carried by a chaplain even as a defensive measure, he or she is seen to be outside the provisions of the Geneva Conventions and, therefore, out of their protection, even though the chaplain is wearing the non-combatant's badge.

Other armed forces may have differing views of this question. My understanding of the American forces is that their chaplains are strictly unarmed as a matter of course, but each will have an armed 'minder' with them wherever and whenever they go. Similarly, my understanding of the British forces is that their chaplains are generally unarmed.

Of course such discussions assume operational units of which chaplains are a part are up against an enemy who has a knowledge of the Geneva Conventions and is willing to respect them. My reading about the current conflict situations existing in the Middle East does not encourage me to think that to be the case there, and thus any consideration of the arming of chaplains and how far into the front lines they may go, has to include deciding the point at which faith and witness become naivety.

These considerations notwithstanding, all Defence chaplains receive weapons training in order to be competent in how they are handled and the safety rules around their use so that, at the very least, they are able to render weapons safe if and when they find themselves ministering among the dead and wounded of a battlefield.

4. Are chaplains legitimizing war by being part of the armed forces?

It may be argued that nothing legitimizes war, for it is a dirty and brutal waste of lives and materials. No one in their right mind would willingly go to war, but such are the complications of life that armed conflict can well be the lesser evil, especially where loss of life, justice and liberty are at stake. That said, a superficial look at the role of the military chaplain would suggest it legitimizes armed conflict; that indeed the Christian Churches have sometimes been complicit in encouraging people to enlist to kill the enemy in times of war, indeed as related earlier, the chaplain's direct role had him at the centre of the battle as he carried aloft his side's 'totem' as the rallying point for the troops and to be an encouragement to them. Today, chaplains can sometimes find themselves manipulated to justify recruitment or to urge troops to greater acts of heroism – but the wise chaplain steers well clear of that, for it is a world away from the direct evangelistic and pastoral role he or she has of supporting the 'flock' in the performance of an unspeakably unpleasant, and dangerous job, and in helping them to see it through in as good a physical, mental and spiritual condition as possible.

This is not always seen in a positive light by the authorities. Lord Kitchener was once moved to write,

> The clergy are the most conservative, tiresome, unimaginative men to deal with that I have ever come across: I suggested all sorts of things to them: proper hymns like "Eternal Father Strong to Save" and "Onward Christian Soldiers", but they would not listen to me: I want this service to be a great recruiting occasion.[1]

4.1. Pros and cons of Chaplaincy

For some Christians, the armed forces are not within the will of God and chaplains therefore should have no part in being a part of them.

---

[1] Underhill M.L., Waters S.D., Ross J.M.S. and Winhall N.E. *New Zealand Chaplains in the Second World War* (War History Branch, Department of Internal Affairs, Wellington 1950).

Such people are right, and they are wrong. They are right in that, in an ideal world, there would be no war, that God's will would be done "....on earth as it is in Heaven..." and that all people, if they had any differences of opinion, would resolve them amicably and without resort to violence. But they are wrong in that the real world is not like that, that it is full of human beings who display all the sinful weaknesses and failings of people everywhere, and it is a world in which sometimes people have to stand up to bad people. As one elderly retired chaplain once said, "I cannot stand by and watch the little guy get hammered!"

For other Christians, insofar as their role as clergy is that of the pastor, and insofar as the military has people in it, then they need pastoring just as much (if not more) than non-military people. They, too, are wrong and they are right. Their error is to think the simple reason of pastoring is sufficient on its own with no further thought given to the morality (*immorality*, if you like) of war.

4.2. The morality of war

An unthinking jingoism does not help any Christian, lay or ordained, to think through the moral complexities of either the morality of war or of being part of an armed military force. God gave us brains and created us as moral creatures who have, or rather should have, a healthy awareness of what is right and what is wrong, so to retreat behind slogans and shallow thinking which owes more to popular trends than to deep thought and careful study, does not bear a faithful witness. In particular, all chaplains have to think through the questions of armed conflict, the application of deadly force and the place of armed forces, as well as to demonstrate a knowledge of 2,000 years of Christian thinking about these issues for, as surely as the sun rises in the East, they will be asked about them, both by civilians and fellow service men and women.

There are no easy answers for, as with many other situations in life, chaplains will be (as the saying has it) 'damned if they do and damned if they don't'. On the one hand, being a uniformed part of an armed force can make chaplains appear complicit in the evils of war. But then can anyone, insofar as most people are taxpayers, claim that they are not: for don't our taxes fund the Armed Forces? Therefore aren't all wage and salary earners tarred with the same brush? Conversely, even when given the complexities of the chaplains' roles, the moral (to say nothing of the literal) minefields that soldiers have to walk through as they bear arms against a foe, Christian love and concern for people place chaplains where they can help their fellow humans go through the unspeakable horrors and traumas of the battlefield and still retain their humanity.

Life's situations can be very complicated and many circumstances can have people facing moral dilemmas for which there are no 'right' or easy answers – and pity help anyone trying to provide them. Humans can often find themselves backed into moral corners in which any action (or inaction) will be open to criticism, especially in the light of subsequent history.

An example is the dropping of the nuclear weapons on the Japanese cities of Hiroshima and Nagasaki in 1945. The critics of this action continue to be heard to this day but, at the time the decision was taken, it was considered the best course of action to end World War II more quickly and with a lesser loss of life than would otherwise have occurred had the alternative (the physical invasion of the Japanese mainland) taken place. The casualties suffered by the American forces during their 'island hopping' campaign through the Pacific, especially the very high numbers killed and wounded in the invasions of Saipan, Iwo Jima, Okinawa *et al*, led them to realise that in the defence of their homeland, the Japanese would have resisted even more fanatically still and would have exacted a terrible toll of life and suffering upon themselves and their foe alike, against which the hastening of the war's end with atom bombs became the lesser of two evils.

5. Is modern war (with its greater destructive capacity) different from that of previous ages?

Again, there is no clear answer. The world has so-called weapons of mass destruction (WMD), meaning that weapons exist which can destroy life (if not property as well) on huge and indiscriminate scales. These are horrific weapons, using either the release of nuclear energy, or of deadly chemicals usually in the form of gas, or bacteriological agents in which a simple test-tube full of microbes could wipe out an entire population. All these destroy every living thing in their path, the 'bonus' of nuclear blasts being that they also flatten buildings and devastate the land whereas chemical and bacteriological warfare simply kill people, leaving buildings intact, though polluted for a time.

The general thinking of the world is to recoil from the use of such weaponry, but that is not to say they haven't been used or never will be. Of course we all know that nuclear bombs were used on the cities of Hiroshima and Nagasaki to bring the war against Japan to an end. With the passage of time, and the change of thinking that accompanies this, this sole example of using nuclear bombs remains controversial. Modern thinkers sometimes contend that such an act was both indefensible and immoral and the United States of America is often criticized for perpetrating this act. On the other hand, as noted already, to the political and military planners of World War Two, such was the demonstrated fanaticism and deadly resistance of the Japanese forces as the Americans fought their way towards Japan, island by island, that it was realistically thought that the cost in dead and in wounded through the direct invasion of Japan itself would be greater than the casualties of a nuclear explosion. Nor is it commonly realized that more people died during the fire-bombing raids on Tokyo than in Hiroshima and Nagasaki.

While there is no recorded use of bacteriological weaponry (and long may this be the case), the last two centuries have seen several examples of the use of chemical warfare. For instance, there are many examples of chemicals being used during World War I where the wind was used to propel clouds of mustard gas towards an opposing army's lines, burning and choking soldiers unless they could don their respirators in time. Such was the fear of chemicals being used again during World War II that Britain's citizens were all issued with gas masks.

Inhumane as the use of gas is, no matter the circumstances, the most recent examples of its use plumbed new depths when they were used against civilian populations, such as the Kurds in Iraq and during the civil war in Syria.

These fearsome and loathsome weapons exist and unfortunately there is no way they can be un-invented. Most people would fervently hope and pray that the last existing examples would be destroyed and reductions in the size of arsenals of such weapons can only be applauded. Well might Christians pray that not only will these weapons vanish from the face of the earth, but that, in the meantime, they do not fall into the hands of extremists of any persuasion.

5.1. The changing face of modern warfare

There is another side to the coin of modern weaponry in that modern delivery systems make conventional arms much more accurate, thus reducing the likelihood of what is these days euphemistically termed as 'collateral damage'. I understand that, statistically, it took something like 800 bombs during World War II to destroy one bridge. Nowadays, so long as some means of 'painting' a target with a laser beam can be used, it takes only one Laser Guided Bomb (LGB) to accurately destroy such a target. One hole in the ground has to be safer and less deadly (especially to non-combatants) than 800.

But it would be a shame if, in our horror of weapons of mass destruction, we inadvertently canonized conventional weaponry. All are designed to kill and to maim, and their use continues to demean humankind. While modern weapons are more precise and accurate than those of yesteryear, those of the 20th and 21st centuries remain the deadliest in world history because the wars in which they have been used have killed or injured more civilians or non-combatants than in the wars of any other time.

In the 'bad old days', wars were relatively localized affairs and usually involved two opposing armies clashing directly with one another on a common battle field. The involvement of non-combatants was consequently much less and, indeed, sometimes these clashes became spectator 'sports' as crowds would come out from nearby cities to watch the two armies slug it out. In more modern times, the North African campaign of World War II is held up as an example of two armies hammering one another in largely unoccupied territory, especially that of the Western Desert.

World War I, by its very title, meant that the entire globe became a potential battlefield. Also, military leadership at that time still used tactics that were once tried and true in the days of mounted cavalry, spears and sabres, but which failed to consider modern inventions such as the machine gun, resulting in massive casualties for very little if any result.

More modern conflicts (Viet Nam being a case in point but the current conflicts in the Middle East also) have resulted in high collateral damage for, while one side is overtly military by virtue of its uniforms and equipment, the other has deliberately blended with the local populace so as to remain invisible within it and, indeed, often sheltering behind it.

A variation of that theme is what is called 'Asymmetric Warfare' or, plain and simple, 'terrorism' in which a combatant deliberately attacks 'soft' targets such as busy train stations, with a view to killing and maiming as many civilians as possible, or else, as graphically displayed on the Internet, will brutally murder essentially innocent people, both to encourage great fear and to exploit the enthusiasm of the media to publicise such events.

6. What about pacifism?

The arguments for pacifism lie principally lie in the Ten Commandments and in the personal example of Jesus. Many, mistakenly citing the seventh Commandment, say "You shall not kill" – when in reality that commandment states, "You shall not murder." While one might wish to argue that the two still add up to the same thing – that no human being has the right to take the life of another – yet in both Old Testament Law and in civil law for centuries Divine and civil justice made provision for capital punishment, not to exact revenge but to maintain justice. While public opinion has spelled the end of capital punishment in most western countries, nonetheless the distinction remains between life taken in passion or criminal act, and that taken as an act of applied justice, be it capital punishment in civil law or killing on a battlefield in the course of a legally declared war.

6.1. Biblical teaching on murder and warfare

To expand this a little further, Exodus 20:13 is translated in the King James Version (KJV) as "Thou shalt not kill", this being the most quoted version of this verse. However, there are nine different Hebrew words that are use 78 times in the Old Testament that are translated as 'kill' in the KJV. The Hebrew word here is 'ratsach' which is translated as 'kill' four times in the KJV but it occurs around 40 times throughout the Hebrew Old Testament. Ratsach is a word that involves killing, but the word implies a personal act of taking someone's life and is variously used to describe manslaughter (Deuteronomy 4:42), revenge killings (Numbers 35:27), assassinations (2 Kings 6:32) and plain old-fashioned murder (Isaiah 1:21 & Hosea 6:9). Taking someone's life for the purpose of personal gain (revenge, robbery, payment, etc) or in a moment of negligence or passion falls more specifically in the categories of murder and manslaughter. This is why a number of translations (eg: New International Version) choose to render Exodus 20:13 as "You shall not murder".

We also need to consider Deuteronomy 20; a whole chapter on the laws of warfare that includes instruction on who the Israelites could and could not kill in war. It includes the direction that in certain cities, it was required that the Israelites "....do not leave alive anything that breathes" (v 16), including men, women, children and animals. Obviously, if God meant that killing in warfare was completely prohibited when he gave the Ten Commandments to Moses, then he would not later contradict himself by giving instructions to kill everything in certain circumstances.

The issue here is not the taking of life, but rather the motivation behind it. People joining the military because they want to shoot people have a serious attitude problem that certainly needs sorting out. They have no place in the military. If, however, a person recognises the need in certain circumstances to defend the innocent and/or the vulnerable from an aggressor, and he or she understands that in carrying out that duty they may need to take someone's life no matter how regrettable, then that person has the right attitude towards military service.

6.2. 'Love your enemies'

Of course, one might object that the law no longer applies to us who live under grace (even though Jesus, quoted in Matthew 5:17 would disagree) and we are now called to live to a higher standard, especially that taught by Jesus in Matthew 5:43-44, "You have heard it was said, 'Love your neighbour and hate your enemy'. But I tell you: Love your enemies and pray for those who persecute you..." This raises the interesting question of whether or not it is possible to love someone as you kill them! Of course military service can well demand that a soldier level his weapon at an enemy soldier and open fire, but Jesus says you must nevertheless love that person you are trying to kill. Here is an example of how Jesus clarified the law: to not murder someone, you need to have removed all personal motivation in that act of killing. This would suggest that a soldier who works himself or herself up into a frenzy of hatred before going into combat is not obeying that 6th Commandment, for we, as Christians, need to act out of necessity and not hatred, anger or revenge. Accordingly, if we are in a situation where, in order to protect others we must kill an enemy soldier who has otherwise not been persuaded to cease and desist, then we can feel compassion and love for that soldier, even though our only option is to open fire.

6.3. Putting theory into practice

That is all very well when considering this question in the comfort of one's home, or study or discussion group etc, but it would feel an entirely different matter out there on the battlefield. We humans possess emotions and feelings so the only dispassionate aspects of any battlefield would be the earth itself and the soldiers' machinery. Facing both armed opposition and a good chance of being killed will not leave any soldier unmoved, no matter how the movies sometimes might want to portray bravery. Of course being on a battlefield will be stressful, of course the adrenalin will be flowing, of course the 'fear quotient' will be very high and of course the soldiers will know that they are in a situation of kill or be killed. The natural stress reactions of 'flight or fight' will be answered only by how well trained and disciplined individual soldiers are and many will testify how, despite their personal terror, they stayed and did what they were trained to do, unspeakable as it was. But to actually and actively love one's enemy in such situations might not be very high in any soldier's priorities and would, I venture, easily be drowned out by the simple and understandable desire to survive.

That's not to say that all human compassion necessarily goes out the window. I remember seeing a photograph taken during the heat of a land battle in the Western Desert during World War II. Two Allied infantry soldiers advancing across the battlefield have come across a badly wounded German soldier. They put aside their weapons for the moment to administer first aid to their enemy, before carrying on with their ordered advance.

Not everything can always be so neat and tidy, though. It was my privilege to know quite well a World War II Spitfire pilot who, after his first aerial combat over France flew back across the channel knowing he had just killed a man, a young man just like him. He related to me how waves of nausea swept over him as he realised the enormity of what he had just done and how he was physically ill in his cockpit. Upon landing and reflecting upon these events, he realised he could not carry on like this and be effective so, to cope, he resolved he would hate his enemy. He said this was not easy to do at first but then, after he was shot down over France and eventually returned to Britain thanks to a loyal French family, he related how, having seen how the Nazis acted as occupiers, how they had shot the daughter of his rescuers in the stomach and thrown her into a cattle car bound for a concentration camp in which she died three days later, he said from that time on, killing Nazis became a pleasure. This was a battle scar this pilot carried for the rest of his life for, while he was a very genial and amusing companion, he carried his hatred, not of Germans so much as of Nazism and those who had sworn allegiance to Hitler, with him to his grave.

6.4. New Testament attitudes

Another aspect of this discussion is Jesus' attitude towards the military. We read in Matthew 8:5-13 about a Roman centurion (as his title suggests, he commanded 100 men) who came to Jesus to ask him to heal his servant. When Jesus offered to go to the centurion's house, he replied he was not deserving of Jesus actually going to his house and surmised that he simply had to command the recovery of the servant and it would be done. After commenting to his followers about the centurion's great faith, Jesus told him to go home for his servant was healed as requested. To give this story some perspective, this Roman was a member of the occupying forces of Rome and, as such, would have been largely detested by the Jews, but Jesus treated him just the same as he treated everyone else and had nothing to say to him about changing his job. While Jesus told tax collectors and prostitutes to go and sin no more, he did not say anything of the kind to this centurion. Well might we ponder, too, the reaction of the Centurion who oversaw Jesus' Crucifixion who, having witnessed our Saviour's death was moved to observe, 'Surely he was the Son of God!'[1]

In his turn, St Paul used the soldier as a positive metaphor of the Christian life, urging Timothy to

> Endure hardship with us like a good soldier of Christ Jesus. No-one serving as a soldier gets involved in civilian affairs – he wants to please his commanding officer.[2]

A further issue is that of conscription or compulsory military service. For Christians, the Bible says they are to be faithful to both God and their country. St Peter, who had seen his Lord handed over to the authorities of his time and crucified, and who had himself been imprisoned by them, nevertheless was inspired to write,

> Submit yourselves for the Lord's sake to every authority instituted among men: whether to the king, as the supreme authority, or to governors, who are sent by him to punish those who do wrong and to commend those who do right. For it is God's will that by doing good you should silence the ignorant talk of foolish men.[3]

---

[1]   Matthew 27:54.
[2]   2 Timothy 2:3-4.
[3]   1 Peter 2:13-15.

For himself, Jesus' personal example was deliberately to decline to defend himself and he only used his power twice to extricate himself from amongst hostile crowds,[4] but only because "...his time had not yet come". While he demonstrated anger towards those who changed money and bought and sold in the Temple when he forcibly cleared them out[5] he nevertheless willingly surrendered himself to the Jewish authorities in the full knowledge that they would put him to death.

6.5. *The ultimate role model*

To me, Jesus was the most secure person who ever trod this earth. He could endure physical hardships and deprivations without complaint,[6] he took personal insults calmly and, while he displayed many miraculous powers, he never used any of them to make himself comfortable. While he could be very biting in his use of words against hypocrisy,[7] his essential message of God's love and grace characterised his teachings to the crowds of ordinary people. But we sometimes tend to make of Jesus a caricature of who He really was with such notions as "Gentle Jesus, meek and mild" which mask the steely resolve that brought him to this earth to live and to die as he did. As Dorothy Sayers wrote,

> The people who hanged Christ never, to do them justice, accused him of being a bore – on the contrary, they thought him too dynamic to be safe. It has been left for later generations to muffle up that shattering personality and surround him with an atmosphere of tedium. We have very efficiently pared the claws of the Lion of Judah, certified him 'meek and mild', and recommended him as a fitting household pet for pale curates and pious old ladies.[8]

Jesus, of all humans, was the most self-possessed. He knew who he was, whom he was here to serve and he kept his eye on the big picture of his purpose here on Earth.

We humans lash out when we are frightened and Jesus was never frightened. We demand the right to defend ourselves but Jesus never

---

4   see Luke 4:30; John 8:59.
5   Matthew 21:13; Mark 11:17; Luke 19:46.
6   eg Matthew 8:20.
7   eg: Matthew 23:13-36.
3   Dorothy Sayers, "The Greatest Drama Ever Staged" *The Whimsical Christian* (Collier Books, 1978) p 14.

did, though He certainly defended others.9 In other words, Jesus was above the petty differences that lead people into war, for He was engaged upon a far greater and more desperate battle against Satan and all that is evil. Would that we weak mortals could be more like Him.

6.6. Problems with Pacifism

Pacifism contends that war is the worst thing in all the world; that nothing, but nothing justifies war; and no human beings should have any part of it, let alone followers of "The Prince of Peace." Yet people would, while deploring war, nevertheless wish to argue that there are worse things happening in this world than armed conflict – injustice, slavery, the abuse of human rights being among them. As I write this, the self-styled Isis caliphate is sweeping across Iraq and demanding people accept their version of Islam's Sharia Law or face an unpleasant death. Reports are reaching the world of people being beheaded and crucified unless they renounce their faith and wholly adopt this ultra-strict version of Islam. That this takes place in the context of an armed invasion of Iraq makes it very difficult for us to stick to a doctrine of non-resistance in the face of this rampant terrorism.

On the other side of the pacifism coin is the complication of the degree to which it should it be held, for there are variations within this general theme and no one fixed philosophical position. For some people, pacifism means not practising *any* form of violence, not being involved in any armed conflict and, indeed, not consenting to enlist in any of the armed forces.

For other pacifists, military service is acceptable but not in combat roles, such service instead to be rendered as medical personnel or as stretcher bearers. However, for some, insofar as that service frees other soldiers for combat, this remains off limits.

But the issue can go beyond this non-involvement. For example, should one sincerely abhor all violence to such a degree as to decline to enlist in or in any other way to aid their country's armed forces? The question still arises in that their taxes help to pay for them. Should they withhold them as well? Of course this is usually not an option, for all citizens who enjoy the state's provisions are obliged to pay their due and lawful taxes and are unable to withhold any portion of them as a protest,

---

9   eg. see John 8:2-11.

or as a way to become further removed from any involvement with military forces, any more than they may withhold taxes in opposition to other aspects of government spending with which they happen to disagree.

Others might wish to argue that there are some conflicts in which the cause can be seen as just and it is therefore permissible for all people actively to support their military forces and enlist in them, whereas other conflicts, not so clear cut, may excuse people from lending their physical support. Unfortunately, such philosophical niceties are not welcomed by governments any more than they would be by military chiefs, charged as they are with raising and maintaining adequate armed forces who will become engaged when ordered to do so, not at the whim of units or the individuals within them.

7. Why Commemorate?

Those who cannot remember the past are condemned to repeat it.

George Santayana (1863 - 1952)[1]

People sometimes question the place of any and all war or battle commemorations. They feel these only glorify war and give veterans an excuse to gather in noisy groups at their clubs, sometimes becoming thoroughly drunk in the process. To them, the stories told and the increasingly raucous laughter that often accompanies them all suggest the 'vets' spent their time in combat having a jolly old time and that their war was a wonderful adventure. They further feel that thinking people should have no part of them.

For Australians and New Zealanders the main commemoration each year is ANZAC Day each April 25. 'ANZAC', an acronym for 'Australian and New Zealand Army Corps' grew out of the early days of World War One when an Allied army, heavily involving troops from both those nations invaded the Gallipoli Peninsula in Turkey in April, 1915.

Without going into the perceived national feelings surrounding this event, ANZAC Day has been commemorated annually since 1916, and while it centres around remembering events of a century ago, its scope has been broadened to include commemorations of all 'Diggers' and 'Kiwis' who died in war. Other countries have their own versions, be they called "Remembrance Day" (11 November in Great Britain, the same day observed as "Veterans Day" in the United States) or "Memorial Day" (United States on the last Monday every May) or whatever. The format appears to follow a set pattern of parades, public commemoration ceremonies consisting of speeches, singing and prayers, and old soldiers gathering to remember comrades living and dead.

Such opinions of these days are not widely shared, indeed, ANZAC Day commemorations in both Australia and New Zealand have seen growing crowds over the past decade, each year's ceremonies being attended by more people than attended the year before, and it appears public appreciation of their significance steadily grows, especially among our nations' young people.

---

[1] George Santayana *The Life of Reason, Vol 1 Reason in Common Sense* (New York: Dover Publications Inc, 1980).

7.1. Collective remembrance and resolve

It is not to glorify war that people gather. While great battles might be specifically remembered, and victories commemorated (to say nothing of such military 'defeats' as the evacuation of Dunkirk and the small invasion at Dieppe during World War II), the overwhelming theme is that of seeking collectively to remember the horrors and waste of all conflicts in order to resolve that war shall be no more.

Thus the common primary aim of commemorations is that of remembrance of deeds done and absent comrades. While ANZAC (25 April) and Remembrance Day (11 November, the end of World War I) might revolve around specific events, the main emphasis is of the waste of war and the sacrifice of human lives. Veterans specifically remember comrades in arms who still lie in foreign fields, families remember relatives and friends, while the population in general is invited to try to envision the horrors of warfare and the cost in blood, misery and grief to those who were directly involved.

It is thus fitting that these commemorations are dignified, solemn affairs which must never be treated perfunctorily or lightly. No one died or otherwise suffered in conflict in order that they either may be forgotten or what they did trivialised.

The solemn words of Laurence Binyon's "Ode for the Fallen" are particularly pertinent, "At the going down of the sun and in the morning, we will remember them" for Santayana's aphorism is all too true.

7.2. Positive lessons

While remembering sacrifice and bloodshed is most appropriate, other aspects of warfare and service in the armed forces are more positive and should also be remembered as lessons for everyday humanity. There is the bonding together of people in a close-knit grouping as they face common hardships, dangers and troubles. For all armed forces personnel, this bonding begins at recruit school where shouting drill instructors are not so much exercising personal power (as many think) as teaching the recruits self-control and personal discipline. The drill instructor is, quite deliberately, 'the enemy' against whom the recruits band together lest that screaming little #^*%* gets the better of them! It is a lesson they will take with them into combat where, despite war films romanticising rugged individualism, teamwork is everything, especially in times of danger.

Another positive of the otherwise negative experience of warfare is the drawing close to comrades in battle, for each soldier knows that his or her comrades are relying on them for protection, just as each individual knows the others are there for him or her. The same applies in the essential teamwork of a ship's company, and of the mutual dependence pilots of an air combat unit have one of another. These bonds become very close, for they are the bonds of ultimate personal sacrifice that a soldier, sailor or aircrew member is prepared to make for the success of the mission or for the lives of the others.

Often, this is not understood. The reality that the bonds of love binding soldiers together can be greater even than family bonds or those between husband and wife can often raise eyebrows. Let's be careful here, for these bonds do not involve any sexual element, but they are of real, self-giving love all the same, and of all human experiences they most nearly approach that *agape* sacrificial love God has for humanity.

Another positive is the technological advances that (especially) major conflicts demand and for which we may be thankful. While we might wearily observe just how ingenious human beings can be when it comes to killing and maiming one another, nonetheless our peacetime world greatly benefits from wartime advances made by such inventions as radar, communications, the treatment of traumatic injuries and aircraft safety systems to name but a few. It is fitting, therefore, that service in a common cause, that advances to aids in modern living which generally are taken for granted, should all feature in commemorations as we thank God for peace and prosperity.

7.3. Positive outcomes

So far, so good, but what should these commemorations then lead to? It is all very well for us to say our prayers, and to make pious pronouncements about sacrifice and service, but what then do we actually *do* about preserving the peace? It follows, then, that commemorations ideally should also encourage people to play their individual parts in preserving the peace we enjoy. Of course this has to begin with being at peace within ourselves and that can come only when we are at peace with God. It is all very well to theorize about the need for world peace and to postulate about how to achieve that, but if individuals aren't at peace within themselves, or prepared to do something about that, then any efforts will be doomed from the start.

From that personal peace then comes commitment to remove the causes of war. Here's where people of all shades and opinions can join together as causes of injustice, unfairness and deprivation are addressed. Of course the task is huge and one may well ask, 'What can one person do?' But that is no excuse to remain idle. One person can do very little, but each person doing a little can add up to an effective whole which can make a noticeable difference to the world. Certainly, there are the Mother Theresas of this world who are well known for their humanitarian work, so, too are such charitable and service organisations ranging from *Medicins sans Frontieres* taking medical help to impoverished areas to *Rotary International* as it tries to eradicate polio around the world. Every country, every town of our western world has its volunteer organisations which aim to alleviate the plight of those less fortunate than themselves. If the will to play a part is there, the channels for doing so are plentiful.

7.4. *Value to veterans*

There are two final points to observe. The first is that the parades of veterans at commemorations are important. No old soldier looks for kudos or public adoration, but recognition and appreciation of what they have done is important. As they march, no matter how frail they may have become, they can hold their heads high, they can feel justifiably proud of their part in the scheme of things and are grateful if the general public can quietly say 'thank you'. My fellow country-men and women are very reticent to display public emotions of any kind, so it is great that as veterans march along the streets on ANZAC Day, the public has begun to clap them as they go by. It makes all the difference to veterans to know they are recognised and their service is appreciated.

The second point is not recognised so easily. As critics of commemorations see the gathering of old soldiers in the Returned and Services Association after the ceremonies, all they observe are a bunch of old geezers telling stories and drinking themselves silly. The value of letting veterans have times together is very important, for they can then tell their stories to people who can relate to them and who understand the context in which they took place. Often families observe that 'Dad never mentioned his war experiences' and sometimes they are hurt by this, for they know there is a story to tell, but 'Dad' often will not tell it to them because, no matter how well he can tell it, and no matter how graphic his words may be, he knows his listeners cannot fully understand what it was like because they were not there at the time. His fellow veterans were and they thus can understand what he is saying and why he is saying it.

To sum up, public commemorations of wartime are good and necessary. They give people a chance to pause and consider how their national and personal history might have changed had not young men and women answered their country's call when it needed them. And they give the population a chance to express their gratitude to veterans, to support their present-day Armed Forces and to feel encouraged to realise that they, too, have a part to play in the preservation of peace.

Commemorations also let the general population see the veterans who live among them and express their thanks and recognition of what they have done. They also let veterans meet so that they can relive their experiences with those who have shared them. Though invisible, the scars of emotional and psychological trauma can be just as real as physical ones but they can last much longer, for decades in many cases, if not for the rest of a veteran's life. In the context of sympathetic and understanding company these invisible scars can gradually heal, too.

Public commemorations are not platforms for criticism of war, particularly of particular events (the Viet Nam war comes to mind), nor are emotional scars healed by personal abuse, criticism or grandstanding at a veterans' event. They don't need reminding of the horrors and wastage of conflict, nor are they looking to remain targets of those upon whom the sad necessity of going to war is lost.

7.5. Attitudes to the enemy

But what of the enemy? Didn't they suffer casualties, too? The answer is obvious for, despite official propaganda, the enemy is human, too. To any soldier the enemy is not portrayed as a fellow human being but as a demon who must be stopped, for wars cannot be fought against a foe who is just like us! There is the well-known incident on the front lines in Europe during World War I when, on Christmas Day, the British and German troops came out of their respective trenches to meet in no man's land to exchange cigarettes and to kick footballs around. If these soldiers had had their way, the war would have stopped there and then, but this would not do, and so their respective hierarchies devoted time and effort into depersonalising the enemy so that the killing could continue.

Once hostilities closed, personal reactions differed. Some immediately built bridges to their former enemies and associated freely with them, while others built walls to keep them apart. I remind you of that highly decorated World War II Spitfire pilot who related his feelings of horror and remorse as he flew back across the English

Channel after his first dogfight and who was physically ill in the cockpit. Right up until the time he died, he carried this hatred within him – yet another unseen scar that few people get to see.

On the other hand, I attended a huge multi-national commemoration in Egypt of the 60th anniversary of the Battle of El Alamein. Representatives of every nation that took part in that battle were there, and I can still hear a senior officer of the British Army acknowledging his former enemies as, 'Good soldiers fighting bravely for a bad cause.'

7.6. Attitudes to life and death

A poem came out of World War II. It has been variously attributed but I first read it as the composition of a Beaufighter pilot flying in the Banff Wing stationed in Scotland:

> Almighty and all-present power
> short is the prayer I make to thee,
> I do not ask in battle hour
> for any shield to cover me.
> The vast unalterable way
> from which the stars do not depart
> may not be turned aside to stay
> the bullet flying to my heart.
> I ask no help to strike my foe,
> I seek no petty victory here;
> the enemy I hate, I know
> to thee is also dear.
> But this I pray: Be at my side
> when death is drawing through the sky,
> Almighty God who also died
> Teach me the way that I should die.[2]

The real enemy is the last enemy described in *The Revelation of St John the Divine* – death. Anything that kills and maims human beings is to be deplored and avoided as much as is humanly possible, but as St Paul

---

[2] Flying Officer E R "Buzz" Davey, 404 Squadron Royal Canadian Air Force, *Extinction (The Airman's Prayer)*, found in the personal effects of Flying Officer Davey after his death in a mid-air collision on 2 October 1944 and believed to have been written by him.

observed, the real foe, the real cause of war, suffering, misery and bereavement is more than human:

> For our struggle is not against flesh and blood, but against the rulers, against the authorities, against the powers of this dark world and against the spiritual forces of evil in the heavenly realms. Therefore put on the full armour of God...[3]

We humans fight against human foes but we are only the tools, the agents, the sinful and visible manifestations of spiritual evil, an evil that would subjugate all humanity under a realm of lies and false promises and which would enslave it to do its will upon earth, even using those who earnestly would pray that God's will be done there instead. As a Flight Sergeant current-affairs lecturer said to a class of Air Training Corps trainees in the very early 1960s,

> Every officer and military leader needs to have not only a Bible, but also a good knowledge of its contents and the will to live as closely as possible to its precepts. Only then will they have the spiritual strength that will enable them to have the physical and psychological strength to withstand all that an enemy would do.

I was in that class but, despite the many years since they were said, those words remain as clear as if they had been said yesterday.

---

[3]   Ephesians 6:12-13a.

8. Serving in today's Armed Forces

If it may be accepted that the existence of Armed Forces is a sad necessity of human life, and remains likely to remain so until the institution of that '...new heaven and a new earth..' testified to by St John in Revelation 21:1, then it follows that they need men and women to serve in them.

8.1. *Clarity on the implications*

As with every other facet of modern living, whether or not a young person should enlist in any armed service needs to be carefully considered with the questions this raises answered before any dotted line is signed. It is all too easy to have a romanticised view of Service life, either for or against, which differs so much from reality that the resulting viewpoint, no matter how sincerely held, is completely wrong. For example, someone who can only see military people as gung-ho, bloodthirsty and champing at the bit to get into conflict if not downright psychopathic, can easily overlook the reality that the average soldier has little interest in facing people shooting at him, but nevertheless can see the positive sides of being part of a force which is able to bring peace and stability to nations and people who know little of either. By the same token, people still enlist into the Army, Navy or Air Force purely with a view to receiving a sound technical training and starting a rewarding career. There is nothing wrong with doing this, so far as this goes, but military service does come with strings attached.

I have known many trainees who started their basic training without having thought through its implications. Some have spent a day or two on the parade ground and have decided this is not for them and so quickly made requests to return to civvy street. For others, the realisation of what military service actually involves has taken longer to sink in. I can remember a young female recruit who sought me out after one of the chaplains' lectures given as part of the basic course. We had pointed out that the Disruptive Pattern Material of their uniforms was practical as camouflage but was by no means a fashion statement for the trendy young, nor was the rifle with which they were issued and which they were learning to use, a toy. No matter what career path they had signed up for, they had to realise that, first and foremost, they were now soldiers of the Queen and, having accepted the Queen's Shilling, they would now do the Queen's bidding. This young lady came to my office in a most indignant frame of mind for, as she put it, she wanted to drive an Air Force fuel tanker and had no intention of carrying a rifle any longer than she absolutely had to and certainly was not willing to even think that she might one day be required to level it at another human being and open fire. She could not or, I rather suspect, would not accept that she was, first and foremost, a soldier of the Queen who might, if world affairs turned out as almost everyone hoped, expect a rewarding and peaceful career but who might equally well be thrown into very confusing and dangerous situations which would demand every ounce of her military training and discipline. That she did not get any of this became loud and clear as she ended her long complaint to me with a prim, "...and besides, those Drill Corporals shout at me and don't say please!"

8.2. Self discipline

Service in the Armed Forces demands discipline. It is a collective discipline that enables bodies of troops to move and work together to achieve a military aim, even though those troops may well face death in doing so. It is their personal or self-discipline that enables them to do this without breaking down or panicking, no matter how terrified they might feel inside. They learn this in every area of their training and subsequent service. Self discipline is learned on the parade ground where they march and drill in unison and where any error is loudly and soundly pointed out. The self discipline comes in when a recruit, especially a physically large one, takes a bawling out by a tiny drill NCO pointing out the trainee's probable ancestry and likely future, with nothing more than a, 'Yes Corporal.' instead of giving way to a personal feeling that he'd really like to drive the Corporal right into the asphalt of the parade ground. It is self discipline and an attention to detail that accepts that even the clothes stacked in a drawer in the bedspace must be laid out in a particular manner, that everything is in its proper order, the socks are so folded and placed that they 'smile' at the inspecting officer and that carefully ironed shirts could be pulled out of their wardrobe and thrown on the floor because they are not considered up to standard.

It is this self discipline that enables a young aircraft mechanic to be patient and meticulous with his or her work on an aeroplane, even to take pride in the excellence with which the job is completed. It is self discipline that enables an Army chef to take pride in the quality of the meals served to the soldier in the middle of the night. It is self discipline that makes a lookout stationed on an exposed upper deck of a warship in a North Atlantic winter's gale maintain a diligent lookout. And it is self discipline that makes a soldier not turn tail and run in the face of an overwhelming enemy, but stand with his or her comrades and fight it out, because they know that only together will they come through the battle.

Somewhere within this process of learning self discipline is the discovery of the pride of achievement, of meeting the required standard, of being part of a large parade in which several dozen, or several hundred well trained troops move together in step and in formation, or of being part of a unit that achieved a military aim against all the odds. Despite an old Battle of Britain pilot once saying to me, "Oh, I just happened to be around at the time with nothing much better to do", such pride is displayed by a studied modesty and nonchalance which covers a much more intense feeling of achievement, even when there are the scars to prove it.

8.3. Intangible benefits

Other intangibles of military life are the comradeship of service together, especially of active service in combat zones, where fellow soldiers learn to rely upon one another and to be absolutely dependable themselves. Many a soldier has testified to how terrified he was when going into battle, but how even more terrified he was of letting his mates down, so he stayed and did his duty. The scorn of comrades was usually enough to keep a soldier at his post, even to the death, rather than the threat of execution for desertion in the face of the enemy. But even in much less dramatic circumstances, the comradeship of having endured some challenges together places people in special relationships to others. For example, I still remember the other members of my Initial Officer Training Course and meeting them is usually always an occasion for more than just the usual exchange of pleasantries and often is an excuse for a little reminiscing.

Another intangible benefit is the identity given a person by their belonging to something that is much greater than themselves. Here is a parable of what it is like to realise that one is a child of God who is loved by Him, even known by name and for whom Christ died. Even the most insignificant and humble of human beings may draw strength and encouragement from this realisation and know he or she has a unique and valued identity – one not for boasting but to be humbly glad about. In the same way, a member of the Armed Forces not only has a uniform to wear but can do so with an inner pride, for they have earned the right to wear it and they can carry themselves proudly. The soldier who puts on his or her uniform each day with pride is a very privileged person.

A more obvious aspect of military life is the education it gives each individual. Once the basic training is out of the way, the trade or professional training begins and this is usually second to none, for the forces work more to a standard than to a price. Even the most humble of Privates or Ordinary Seamen or Aircraftmen or women have a part to play in the effective operation of the whole, and so their training aims to make them capable at a world standard, conscientious in their duties and appreciative of their place in the grand scheme of things. As the ancient proverb has been telling us for centuries, "For the want of a nail.....the battle was lost!" so is every trainee taught that what they do, and the way in which they do it *does* matter!

Given that chaplains are missionaries in uniform all the above present golden opportunities for them to encourage service men and women to be thankful to God for giving them strength to do both their ordinary and extra-ordinary duties, especially those in dangerous places or circumstances. Also to be thankful that God has delivered them and, even for battle casualties, this is a sign of the greatest deliverance ever provided to humanity by a gracious God who offers eternal life to all at the greatest cost to Himself. As Jesus Himself observed, 'Greater love has no-one than this: that he lay down his life for his friends.'[1]

---

[1] John 15:13.

9. Should we encourage clergy to become chaplains?

There is a short answer to this question. It is, "Yes, but only if they are good!" Indeed, only if they are the best.

The bane of a senior chaplain's life is a friendly telephone call from a Bishop along the lines of, "there is a cleric in the Diocese whose talents don't really suit him/her to parish life and I *really* think their becoming a chaplain to the forces is just what they were ordained for!" I know I can be cynical, but what the Bishop is really saying is this cleric is hopeless and he would be glad to be shot of him or her. What better place for them than the Armed Forces where he or she will be out of sight and out of mind! Problem solved! Add to this scenario the view held by some people that 'those who can are parish clergy while those who can't become chaplains...' and one can begin to see that even within Church circles, chaplaincy in general and military chaplaincy in particular are not necessarily highly thought of. Indeed, military chaplains can be attacked from both Christian and secular sides, as wryly commented upon by Francis Quarles (1592 – 1644):

> Our God and Souldiers we alike adore,
> Ev'n at the Brink of danger; not before.
> After deliverance, both alike requited;
> Our God's forgotten, and our Souldiers slighted.[1]

9.1. A unique mission field

The military is a unique mission field. In it are 'all sorts and conditions of men' (and women) just as in the civilian world, but in the military they live and work together in very close proximity. If you like, an armed service is like a large business corporation which has invited clergy to be a part of its support team and which employs them to attend to the physical and spiritual welfare of its personnel, especially when they are required to go to unpleasant places to do very dangerous jobs.

The Armed Forces need chaplains and they have a long history of making a place for them in their organisations and, insofar as they are

---

[1]   Ed. Alexander B Grosart , *Of Common Devotion. The complete works in Prose and Verse of Francis Quarles* (Edinburgh: T. and A. Constable, 1880), Volume 2, p 205.

there to minister to everyone, no matter what their place in the organisation may be, or what spiritual enthusiasm they may (or may not) have, they can devote themselves fully to rubbing shoulders with everyone. Chaplains, if you like, are missionaries who are paid to meet and minister to all service persons at their places of work. Those people have needs that all people have as they try to cope with everyday living and in that regard, the duties of a military chaplain will contain most of those he or she had in civilian life with the possible exceptions of the administration and the financing of a parish.

But added to these are the needs arising from the pressures of service living, be they the homesickness of a new recruit, a divorce influencing the concentration of a fitter working on an ejection seat, a young mum trying to cope at home when her husband went to sea with the keys to the family car still in his pocket, or sitting with a soldier who has just returned from a combat where his best mate was killed.

9.2. A pastoral heart

All these people need pastoral support from someone competent to provide it, with the skills to impart it and who have the compassion of our Saviour which takes them well out of their comfort zones of physical location or feelings of professional ability. While most Armed Forces have their Social Workers, Family Support Officers and other welfare staff, there remains a special and unique place for the Man or Woman of God who can take people in need beyond providing for their physical situations, or their feelings of self-worth, and into the realms of their place in the universe and in the eyes of the Living God who loves them. Even very irreligious people will derive comfort from knowing that they have access to a person whose motivation goes well beyond the need to earn a living or to do something worthwhile in the world, who is openly and genuinely demonstrative of their compassionate willingness to be their friend who understands their situation and is there for them. That this 'friend' wears the same uniform, is fully understanding of the system in which they live – indeed, is a recognised and affirmed part of it – only adds to the worth and place of the chaplain.

I served under a Group Captain commander of a base where I was the chaplain. He was an avowed atheist ("I have looked but I just don't see anything there.") but that didn't stop him being one of the most supportive Commanding Officers any chaplain could wish for. I remember the powerful arguments he wrote to the Personnel Branch in support of adding to the establishment of chaplains on his base, and how he said once, "While the chaplains are not the most valuable of my officers, I can think of many I am prepared to do without before I would be prepared to do without my chaplains!"

Or as General Bernard Montgomery famously declared in Cairo Cathedral during World War II, "I would as soon think of going into battle without my artillery, as without my chaplains!"

9.3. A practical heart

This story came from the World War II Battle for Crete. The British and Commonwealth troops were ordered to evacuate the island but to do so involved a long, hot, dusty trek in bright sunshine across a high pass to the south coast of the island where the Royal Navy waited for them. At the top of the pass, General Freyberg of the New Zealand Division was watching his weary troops walk past as they started down the other side towards the embarkation beaches. A chaplain walked past and, seeing he had several water bottles slung over his shoulders, the General, a little caustically asked him if he was suffering from thirst. The chaplain turned to his General and, ignoring the implied slight, answered that a lot of the troops had no water and were suffering terribly. It was then that the General noticed that the chaplain was covered in dust and his lips were cracked and dry. The chaplain hadn't touched a drop, all the water he carried was for his troops.

I have already mentioned World War I chaplain Geoffrey Studdart-Kennedy who was a constant sight to the British troops in the trenches of France. While many of his fellow chaplains kept themselves mostly in the comforts of Officers' Messes behind the front lines and well out of artillery range, chaplain Studdart-Kennedy, with his uniform pockets stuffed full of packets of cigarettes would be walking the trenches and so freely handing them out, that he earned for himself the enduring affectionate nickname of "Woodbine Willy".

As the motto of the Royal Air Force's chaplains explains, chaplains are in uniform *Ministrare non Ministrari* – "To Serve not be Served."

9.4. A heart for Jesus

The primary qualification for any chaplain is that she or he is totally, unreservedly in love with Jesus Christ as Saviour, friend and brother. The relationship must be strong and enduring and fed daily by Bible reading and prayer, for nothing less will enable that chaplain adequately to fulfil the task ahead and to have the strength to endure. The calling is no sinecure, for even in the everyday routine of military life there will be most of the tasks of administration and management done by any parish clergy, but added will be the particular demands and hazards of military duty. These latter can include everything from writing a prayer to use on a ceremonial parade such as a recruit graduation, to teaching a class of senior non-commissioned officers the rudiments of pastoral care, to sitting with a young wife whose husband's plane has just crashed and she doesn't yet know if he is still alive, to visiting sentries standing lonely guard in the pouring rain at 0200 hrs.

The demand, therefore, is for one who is spiritually secure, who enjoys not only a close and personal relationship with God but also has been given the eyes of God's grace and compassion in order to sit with people as they endure all that life throws at them. Insofar as chaplains are friends and advisers to all military personnel, they need to know that their feet stand on the firmest of foundations. Thus a chaplain needs to have the devotion, along with the personal commitment and self discipline to have and to maintain a very strong devotional life of daily prayer and Scripture reading, of study and meditation upon what God's Word says and a prayerful awaiting upon what God would have them do.

9.5. Physical and emotional strength

Along with this spiritual fitness must go physical fitness. All military personnel are required to be fit and to verify that fitness regularly with the various exercises and fitness tests each Service has. The chaplain need not think he or she is exempt from these, for not only must they be able to keep up with the members of their respective flocks, but it is important for their personal credibility that they are seen doing so. The chaplain who becomes better known for being forever in the office or hiding in the comfortable confines of the Officers' Mess will not gain the respect of fellow servicemen or women. When the soldiers are marching through the bush in the rain, the chaplain must also march through the bush in the rain with them. If an Air Force unit is undergoing an all-night training exercise, the chaplain is out there with them. If the mess deck of a naval vessel heaving its way through heavy seas has become a scene of sickness and injury, then that is the duty station of the ship's chaplain. The identification of any chaplain goes far beyond their simply wearing the same uniform, important and all as that is, and it goes well beyond any chaplain's desire for personal comfort to ensure that he or she is out there with the troops and by every means possible, ensuring their welfare.

Add to this mix the chaplain's need for high mental and emotional strength. Identifying with the lot of the troops does not mean breaking down with those who are reaching the end of their emotional rope, nor does it mean that the chaplain should lead the tactical withdrawal or the evacuation. It means being strong when others are about to give in to their fears, it means remaining calm at times of great noise, confusion and danger, it means remaining firm and dependable. As Rudyard Kipling in his poem "If" put it, "If you can keep your head when all around are losing theirs...."

In other words, the chaplain should be the last person standing. He or she is to be the rock that remains, and they can only be this because they rely upon their 'Rock' – God Himself.

9.6. Courage

Bear in mind, courage is not the absence of fear. Most mortals know what fear is, but it is courage which drives us on despite our fears. As someone once put it, 'Courage is when you and God are the only ones who know just how scared you really are!'

As well as this physical courage, the chaplain also needs moral courage, that courage which stands firm for principle and fairness and what is right. It was this moral courage which sent a fuming navy chaplain to the Captain of a large naval vessel to confront him with his selective morality. It is this moral courage which sees a chaplain sit down with a Commanding Officer to tell him, "Sir, that is wrong!" It is moral courage when the chaplain who said grace at the beginning of a formal dinner becomes so appalled at the drunken and licentious behaviour of his fellow diners as the dinner progresses, that he leaps to his feet and shouts over the clamour to the Mess President that this was not what he had in mind as he asked God to bless the meal and the occasion.

It was this same moral courage demanded of the prophet Ezekiel when God sent him to admonish the people:

And whether they listen or fail to listen – for they are a rebellious house – they will know that a prophet has been among them.[2]

---

[2]   Ezekiel 2:5.

Moral courage, no less vital than physical courage, means being willing to sacrifice personal popularity and comfort for what is right. While, sometimes, people will not necessarily like it, they will nevertheless respect those who display it.

These are the qualities of the chaplain. Those who like comfort, those who are defined by uniforms and badges of rank, those who are unsure of their calling or who think being ordained is a cushy number, those who have little time for people especially the hurting people of this life and those who are not prepared to go the extra mile on behalf of his or her troops need not apply, for not only will they be non-effective, they will be unable to cope.

It's not a job for sissies!

10. Designing Commemorations

Whether they are chaplains, former chaplains or civilians, clergy (laity too) can expect to be asked both to assist with the setting up of commemorations and to take part in them. This can happen at any time, especially near the dates of significant military events and regular observances such as Remembrance Day, but such invitations are much more likely now that World War I began just over 100 years ago. For the next four years at least there will most likely be an increased tempo of these commemorations so here follows a small collection of 'tools' which may help with preparations for, and the conduct of, public ceremonies, as well as those requested by organisations associated with individual units, squadrons and ships etc.

No matter how large or (especially) how small these may be, all should be taken very seriously, for they are great pastoral and teaching opportunities within which to bear a faithful witness to Jesus Christ. Yes, while it might be easy to dismiss the motives of the gawking multitudes who attend large ceremonies, remember that some spirit of inquiry and a sense of occasion has brought them along. Also, that within their midst will be the veterans for whom these times are particularly significant. Whether the veterans parade as part of a large gathering, or whether they comprise the whole of a unit reunion, being able to recall past experiences and to remember former comrades will be very moving for them. Never take these opportunities lightly or allow your performance within them to become perfunctory.

10.1. Structure

The usual elements of such events will involve someone who acts as Master of Ceremonies, a Guest Speaker, a Bible Reading, maybe read extracts from other writings, and prayers. Also, they usually contain the recitation of Binyon's "Ode" as well as the playing of the Last Post and the Reveille, the placing of poppies and wreaths with or without a minute or two's silence.

A typical format might look like this:

1.   Welcome
2.   Statement of what this event is for
3.   An opening prayer
4.   Bible Reading

5. Guest Speaker
6. Selected reading from a unit or war history
7. Prayers of remembrance, thankfulness and for peace
8. Wreath laying
9. The Last Post is played
10. Binyon's 'Ode'
11. The Reveille is played
12. Placing of poppies
13. Benediction

Of course this list is not exhaustive and those arranging a commemoration are free to include and exclude whatever they feel will be appropriate to the occasion, as well as to arrange the order to suit. There is no one, right and proper order or content, the above simply being a suggestion and an indication of what usually takes place; but as occasions, circumstances and people all differ, so too can these ceremonies – so one designed for an Abbey, Minster or other large Church will differ from that of a large parade at the city Cenotaph which will, in turn differ from that of a small town, or a squad of soldiers standing with their weapons under a clump of palm trees or under the desert sun.

10.2. Prayers

The Prayers may contain the following elements:

1. *Remembrance*
❖ Of events in days gone by;
❖ Of the suffering and the wastage of war;
❖ Of the cost in human lives and dignity.

2. *Repentance*
❖ For the human propensity for going to war;
❖ For an inability to settle differences amicably;
❖ That we are sinful people before God.

3. *Thankfulness*
❖ For the current peace and freedom we enjoy;
❖ For the positive features of military service such as comradeship, close bonds of service and the satisfaction of working towards a common goal;

- ❖ For the accelerated progress of science during wartime which goes on to have beneficial peacetime applications;
- ❖ To God for life;
- ❖ To God for His Son, our Saviour;
- ❖ For those who went to war to secure our peace;
- ❖ For those who gave their lives;
- ❖ For the current personnel of the armed forces.

4. *Intercessions*
- ❖ For current serving personnel, especially those on operations;
- ❖ For their families, particularly those that have to cope alone;
- ❖ For our Queen, her governments and all world leaders;
- ❖ For the United Nations;
- ❖ For those who continue to bear the physical, emotional and psychological scars of their service;
- ❖ For ourselves, that we might be at peace with God, with ourselves and with one another.

5. *Blessing or Benediction*
- ❖ For us and for all humanity

I would offer the suggestion that, in most contexts, and given that such commemorations are usually public events with people of all religious persuasions (and none) present, the prayers should not be long, sonorous or full of old language or Christian jargon. If we can pray 'in the language understanded of the people' (but without the swearing!) then they may feel encouraged to add their own "Amen" to ours. Language and similes etc they don't understand only reinforce in their minds that Christians are too heavenly minded to be of much earthly use and the divide between them and God will only widen.

But, if with our prayers and other words, we can speak *for* ordinary men and women, and can do so without any loss of dignity or decorum that commemorations properly demand, then we are beginning to bridge the gap as people then have a chance to see that being a Christian, and talking to God is the most natural thing that human beings can do.

10.3. Resources

Binyon's 'Ode'
> They shall grow not old
> As we that are left grow old.
> Age shall not weary them
> Nor the years condemn.
> At the going down of the sun
> And in the morning,
> We will remember them.

Laurence Binyon (1869 – 1943)

Finally, here is a beautiful prayer used in an English Church in November, 2014. It is typical of all that I have tried to say in this chapter:

Heavenly Father,

On this Remembrance Sunday we thank you for the courage and the bravery of all the men and women who serve and have served in the military.

We pray especially for those who will find Remembrance Day hard as they grieve the loss of loved ones.

We pray too for all those who have been injured through war, and are still fighting either physically or mentally.

We thank you for those who have laid down their lives for us so that we can live in peace and free from fear.

Today as every day we thank you especially for the ultimate sacrifice of the Lord Jesus who laid down his life for us to bring us peace with you.

In Jesus' Name.   Amen

If you have enjoyed this book, you might like to consider

- *supporting the work of the Latimer Trust*

- *reading more of our publications*

- *recommending them to others*

See www.latimertrust.org for more information.

LATIMER PUBLICATIONS

LATIMER PUBLICATIONS

Latimer Publications

Lightning Source UK Ltd.
Milton Keynes UK
UKOW02f2159010515

250760UK00002B/21/P